W9-AVI-865

LITTLE MOUSE'S LEARN-AND-PLAY

Colors

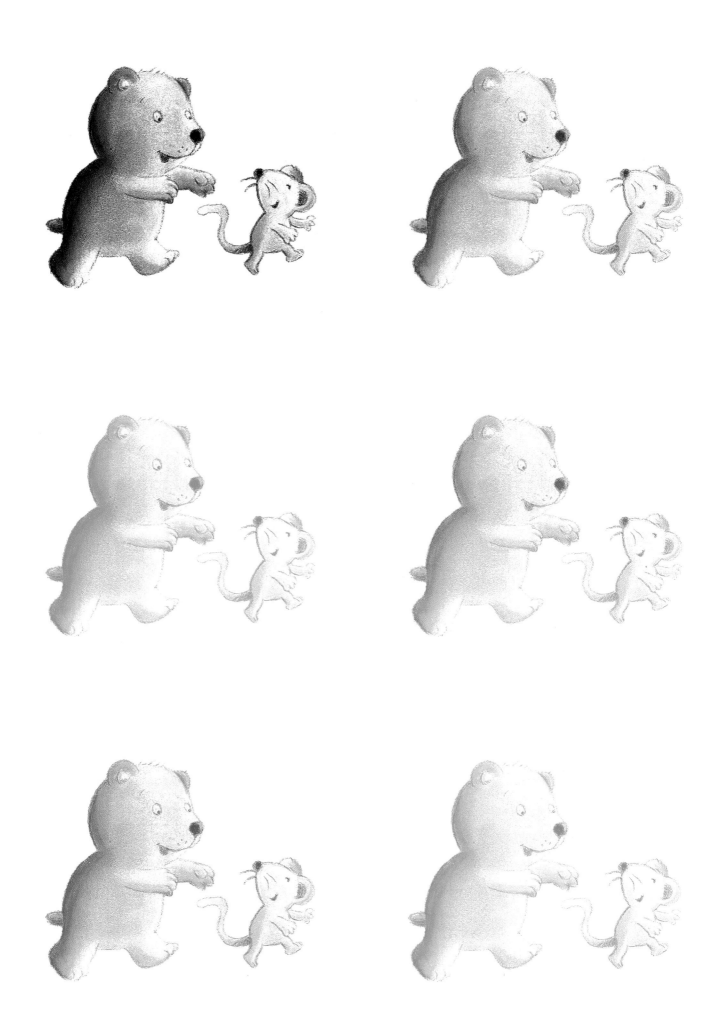

For a free color catalog describing Gareth Stevens' list of high-quality books and multimedia programs, call 1-800-542-2595 (USA) or 1-800-461-9120 (Canada). Gareth Stevens Publishing's Fax: (414) 225-0377.
See our catalog, too, on the World Wide Web: http://gsinc.com

Library of Congress Cataloging-in-Publication Data

Dena, Anaël.
   [Couleurs. English]
   Colors / text by Anaël Dena ; illustrated by Christel Desmoinaux.
      p. cm. — (Little Mouse's learn-and-play)
   Summary: Text, art, and activities introduce red, blue, yellow, and
other colors.
   ISBN 0-8368-1984-5 (lib. bdg)
    1. Colors—Study and teaching—Activity programs—Juvenile literature.
[1. Color.] I. Desmoinaux, Christel, ill. II. Title. III. Series: Dena, Anaël.
Little Mouse's learn-and-play.
QC495.5.D46 1997
535.6—dc21   97-20901

This North American edition first published in 1997 by
Gareth Stevens Publishing
1555 North RiverCenter Drive, Suite 201
Milwaukee, Wisconsin 53212 USA

This U.S. edition © 1997 by Gareth Stevens, Inc. Original © 1994 by Editions Nathan, Paris, France. Titre de l'edition originale (original title): *Les Couleurs* publiée par Les Editions Nathan, Paris. Additional end matter © 1997 by Gareth Stevens, Inc.

Translated from the French by Janet Neis.
U.S. editors: Patricia Lantier-Sampon and Rita Reitci
Editorial assistant: Diane Laska

All rights reserved. No part of this book may be reproduced, stored in a retrieval system, or transmitted in any form or by any means, electronic, mechanical, photo-copying, or otherwise, without the prior written permission of the copyright holder.

Printed in the United States of America

1 2 3 4 5 6 7 8 9 01 00 99 98 97

LITTLE MOUSE'S LEARN-AND-PLAY

Colors

by Anaël Dena
Illustrations by Christel Desmoinaux

Gareth Stevens Publishing
MILWAUKEE

j535.6
DEN

Red

Little Bear wakes up.

He yawns and stretches.

Rise and shine, Little Bear!

A new day is beginning.

Look at all the **red** things above. Can you find them in the big picture?

Blue

Little Bear is taking a bath.

He loves to play in the water.

Soon he is clean from

head to toe.

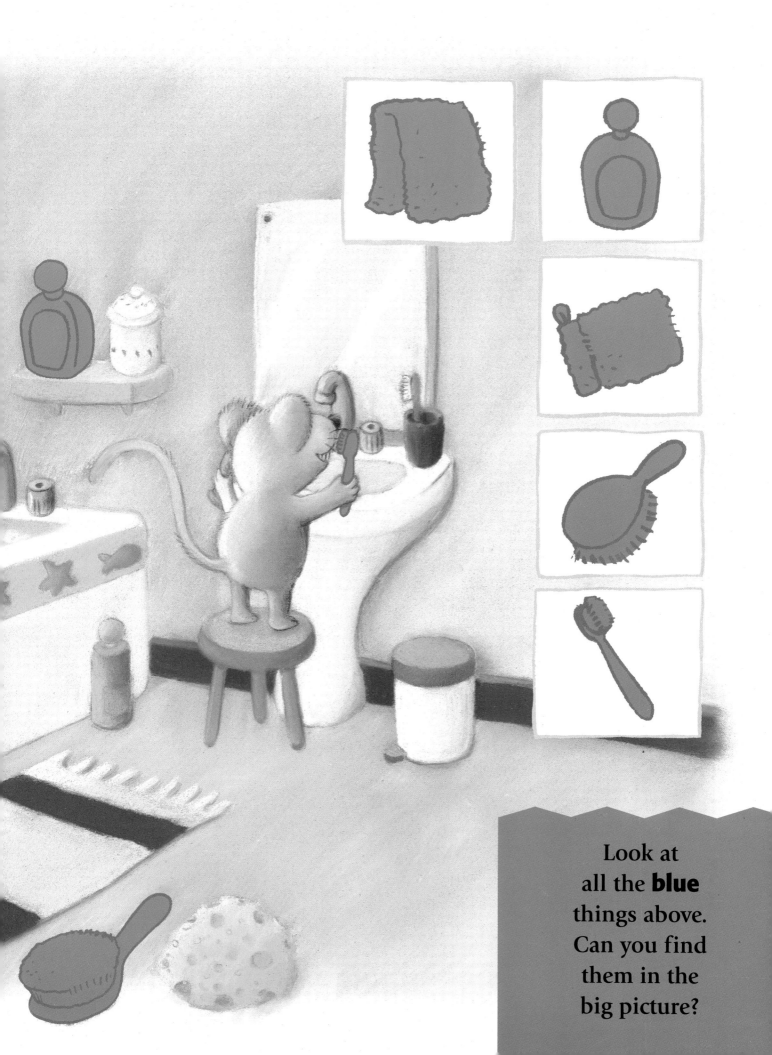

Look at
all the **blue**
things above.
Can you find
them in the
big picture?

Yellow

Little Bear puts on his socks,
his shirt, and his overalls.
When he is dressed, he
will go out to play.

Look at
all the **yellow**
things above.
Can you find
them in the
big picture?

Orange

Little Bear is very hungry.
He puts on his apron and
makes a delicious lunch.

Look at all the **orange** things above. Can you find them in the big picture?

Green

Little Bear works in
his garden every day.
He takes good care of his
plants so they grow well.

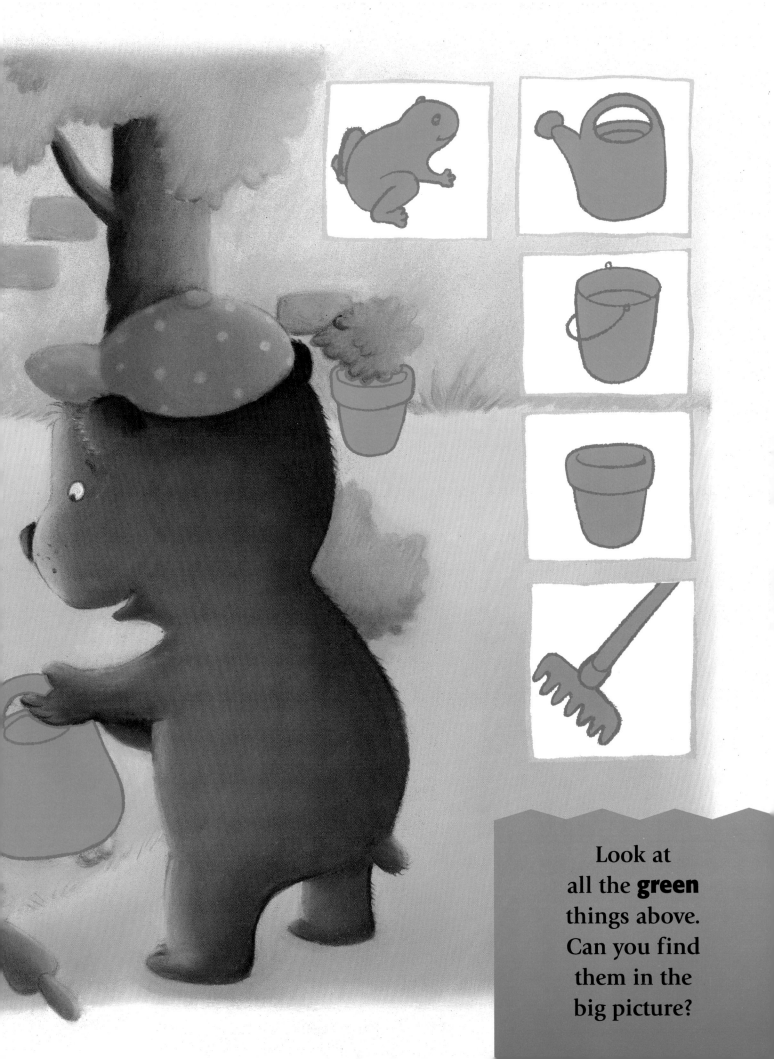

Look at all the **green** things above. Can you find them in the big picture?

Pink

Little Bear rests

from his hard work.

He sits on his cozy couch

and enjoys a little snack.

Look at all the **pink** things above. Can you find them in the big picture?

Little Bear puts on a magic show for his friends. His tricks amaze them all. They clap and clap.

Look at all the **black** things above. Can you find them in the big picture?

White

It snowed early this morning!
Little Bear quickly bundles
up and goes sledding
down the hill.

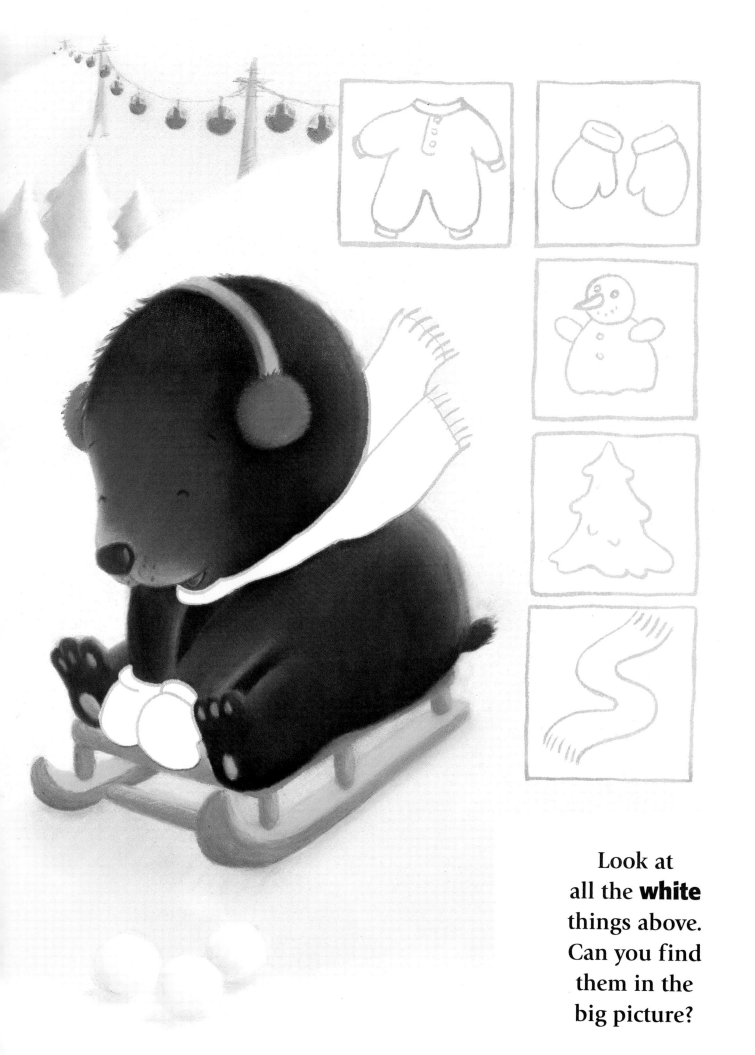

Look at all the **white** things above. Can you find them in the big picture?

Here are some more colors!

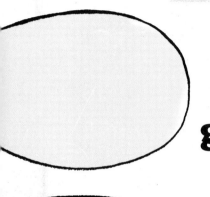 **gray**  like an elephant.

 **brown**  like a bear.

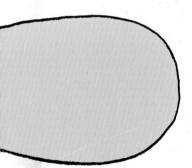 **tan**  like a sweater.

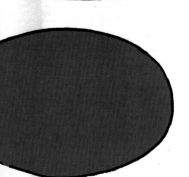 **purple**  like an eggplant.

Can you tell which things are **gray, brown, tan**, or **purple**?

Transparent

Things you can see
through are transparent,
or clear.

Can you find
anything **transparent**
in this picture?
Can you find
something that
is not **transparent**
that reflects people
and things?

The two-color game

The bear cubs are playing.
Each bear wears two colors
that another bear is wearing.

Can you match
up the two bears
that wear the
same colors?
Where is Little Bear?
He is wearing
blue pants and
a **pink** shirt.

The three-color game

Let's go for a walk. Don't forget
to take along your favorite toys!

Each bear cub has two toys the same colors as its clothes. Can you match the toys with their owners?

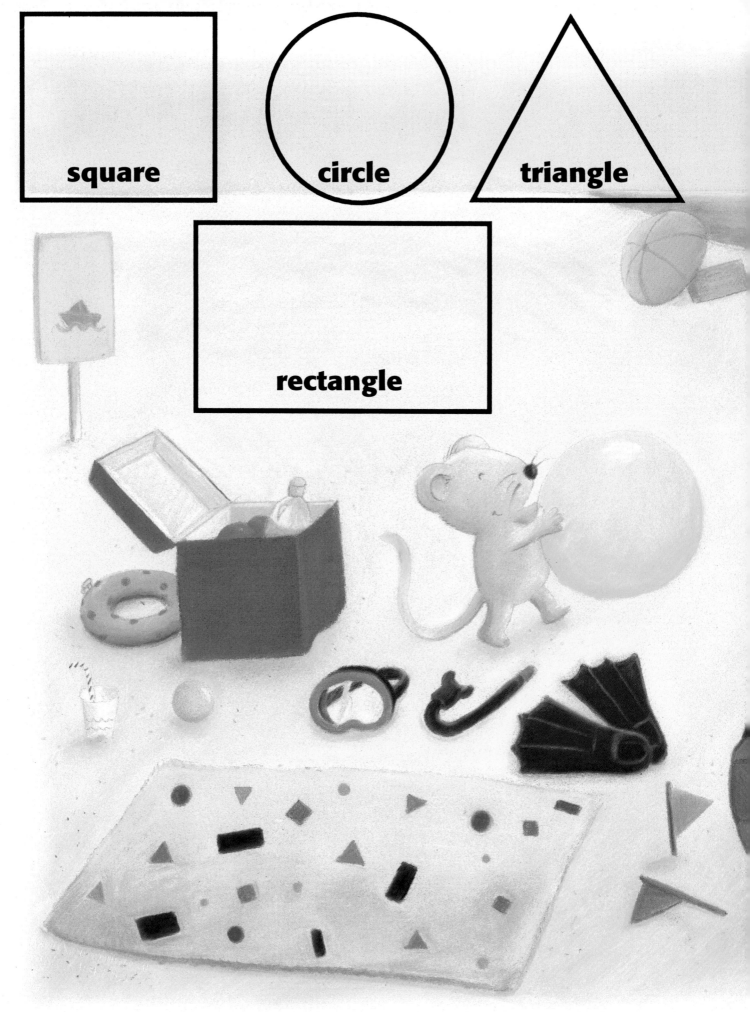

square

circle

triangle

rectangle

Find the **squares**
in this picture.
Next find the **circles**,
the **triangles**,
and the **rectangles**.
Can you find an **orange
square**? Now look
for a **yellow circle**,
a **blue triangle**, and
a **black rectangle**.

 **spots**  **stripes**

Which animals
have **spots**?
Which have **stripes**?
Can you match each
animal with its baby?

C checks

P polka dots

Z zigzags

W waves

Find things in this picture that have **checks**, **polka dots**, **zigzags**, or **waves**.

Nature changes colors!

Spring

Summer

Autumn

Winter

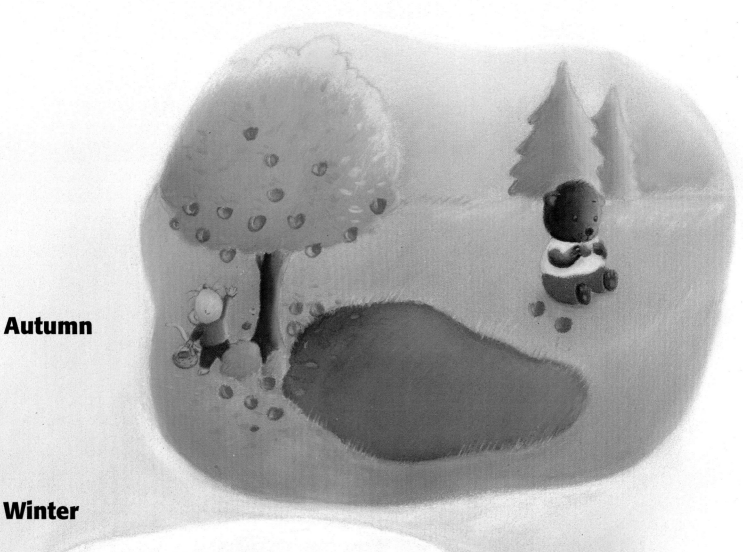

What things change color in each picture? Can you find anything that stays the same color in every season? Look at the tree trunk! What else does not change color?

What things are the same color? Can you find the same two things that are different colors? Can you find the same two things that are the same color?

Memory game

Play this game with everything you see on this page and the next. Look carefully at all the objects on the table. When you think you can remember everything, turn the page.

The bear cubs have changed
some things on the table.
Which objects have changed color?
Which objects have changed places?
Which two objects have disappeared?

Can you find some objects
that are in the same place and
are the same color?

Turn back one page and check the
table. Did you forget anything?

The Little Painters

You can mix colors to make other colors. Look at the color circles below. What colors did the bear cubs mix to paint each toy?

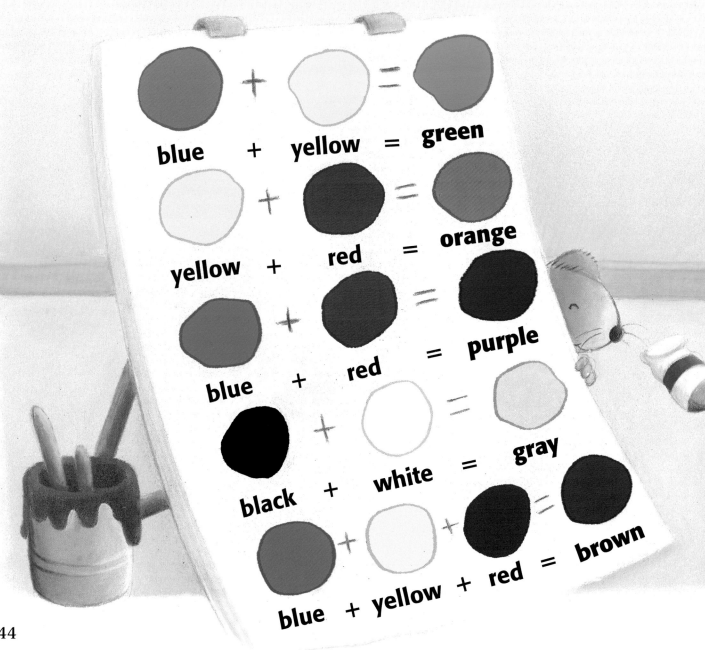

blue + yellow = **green**

yellow + red = **orange**

blue + red = **purple**

black + white = **gray**

blue + yellow + red = **brown**

Books

Colorful Light. Julian Rowe and Molly Perham (Childrens Press)

Colors Everywhere. Tana Hoban (Greenwillow)

Discover Colors. Marie-Agnes Gaudrat and Thierry Courtin (Barron)

Little Giants series. Alan Rogers (Gareth Stevens)

Mandarins and Marigolds: A Child's Journey through Color. Diz Wallis (Gareth Stevens)

My Book of Shapes and Colors. (Penguin)

My Colors. Faulkner. (Simon and Schuster Children's)

Naming Colors. Ariane Dewey (HarperCollins Children's)

Projects with Color and Light. (Gareth Stevens)

Rummage Sale: A Fun Book of Shapes and Colors. Neil Morris (Lerner Group)

The Science of Color series. Barbara J. Behm and Donna Bailey (Gareth Stevens)

The Secret of the Hawaiian Rainbow. Stacy S. Kaopuiki (Hawaiian Island Concepts)

Videos

Art for Beginners: Fun with Lines. (Coronet, The Multimedia Co./ MTI Film and Video)

Color, Color Everywhere — Red, Yellow, Blue. (Coronet, The Multimedia Co./MTI Film and Video)

Colors. (Good Apple)

Colors All Around Us. (AIMS Media)

Colours. (Superior Promotions)

Web Sites

www.bonus.com/
(*See* Parents & Teachers, Fun for Young Kids, I Spy, Vector images, Compass picture, Basic Shapes)

www.ravenna.com/coloring/

Glossary – Index

amaze: to fill with wonder; to puzzle someone (*p. 18*).

apron: a large piece of cloth or leather tied around the waist to protect clothing (*p. 12*).

bundle up: to dress warmly (*p. 20*).

check (*v*): to examine or compare (*p. 42*).

clap: to strike the hands together noisily to show liking or approval for something (*p. 18*).

couch: a wide piece of furniture for sitting or lying down (*p. 16*).

cozy: comfortable; snug (*p. 16*).

delicious: pleasant; very tasty (*p. 12*).

different: not the same (*pp. 38, 39*).

disappear: to go out of sight (*p. 42*).

favorite: something that is liked more than the others (*p. 28*).

garden: a small piece of land where vegetables or flowers are grown (*p. 14*).

magic show: a show in which someone does tricks that appear to be due to special powers, or magic (*p. 18*).

match (*v*): to find or choose things, such as socks or shoes, that belong together (*pp. 27, 29, 33*).

nature: the natural workings of Earth (*p. 36*).

overalls: a pair of shorts or pants held up by straps (*p. 10*).

reflect: to show back an image or likeness (*p. 25*).

season: a period of the year that has a particular kind of weather. The four seasons are spring, summer, autumn, and winter (*p. 37*).

snack: a small amount of food eaten between meals (*p. 16*).

transparent: letting light pass through so things on the other side can be seen; clear (*pp. 24, 25*).